The Godtouch

Stephen R. Clark

Epiphany Lane™ Press • Oreland, PA

The Godtouch

Copyright © by Stephen R. Clark

All rights reserved.

All the characters in this book are fictitious, and any resemblance to actual persons living or dead is purely coincidental. No part of this book may be reproduced or transmitted in any form or by any means, electronic or mechanical, including photocopying, recording, or by any information storage and retrieval system, without permission in writing from the publisher.

Original versions published in 1985 & 2004

2017 ELP Edition

Epiphany Lane™ is a trademark owned by Stephen R. Clark

Dedication

To
The most special loved ones in my life,
Sis, Michael, BethAnn, and my many friends;
And to the memory of my beloved parents,
Walter and Grace.

Soli Deo Gloria

Contents

Introduction, *11*

First Words (Original Foreword), *15*

Part One :: The Forgetting Season
The Forgetting Season, *19*
Love, Wind & Innocence, *20*
Thumbs & Pulses, *21*
Withstanding the Storm, *22*
Last Days, *24*
Rounds, *25*
Tangled in Time, *26*
The Prankster: A Memorandum, *27*
Afternoon, Fading, *28*
Fear & Loafing, *29*
Shut the Door Behind You, *30*

Part Two :: The Christmas Poems
Love Poem, *33*
The Star, *34*
The Shepherds, *36*
The Angels, *38*
The Nativity, *39*
The Wisemen, *41*
The Fool, *42*
Prayer at Midwinter, *43*
Watching Snow, *44*
Winter, Snow & Cold, *45*

Part Three :: Seasonal Hell

Seasonal Hell, 49

Greeting & Confirmation, 50

Remodeling, 51

Backyards: Summer: Night, 53

Night Sketch: Heat & Rain, 54

Night as Child, 55

The Fear of God, 56

Advertising, 59

Part Four :: Easter Poems

The Runner, 63

Christ Came Down, Arising, 64

The Betrayal, 65

The Shining, 66

The Taking, 68

The Point, 69

Wood to Flesh, 70

First Easter Morning, 71

Cleansing of the Temple, 72

Part Five :: The Hunt

The Hunt, 75

God Even Gideon, 76

Relocation, 77

Dry Tinder Quenched, 78

Laughing Savior, 79

The Incoming, 80

Maintenance, 81

Hymn, 83

Praise, 84

Masonry, 85

Part Six :: Leavings

Leavings, 89
Recovery, 90
Moment Of Always Meeting, 92
In Silence Singing, 94
A Step is not a Leap, 96
The Sickness, 97
The Godtouch, 98

Part Seven :: More

Wound, 103
Bad Ending, 104
Dreamsong / Nightsong, 105
When Night Falls, 106
Some, 107
Christmas Trinity, 108
Nice Ice, 109
Epiphany Eidolic, 110
Affirmations Against Aloneness, 111
Clue, 112
Misfit, 113
If, Then, Instead, 114
Tears of Fire, 115
The Secret of Being, 117
Roads, 118
Pied Piper, 119
A Lecture on Advanced Writing Techniques, 120
Together. Very., 122
With All My Strength, 123
It Rattles, 124
Hearts of Steel, 125

Haiku Ramblings, *126*
- Cicada I, *126*
- Cicada II, *126*
- Cicada III, *126*
- Cicada IV, *126*
- Cicada V, *126*
- Cicada VI, *126*
- Divorce I, *127*
- Divorce II, *127*
- Divorce III, *127*
- Divorce IV, *127*
- Arguing, *127*
- Forsaken, *127*
- Change, *127*
- Spam, *128*
- Spring Tease, *128*
- Reticence, *128*

About the Author, *129*

Also by Stephen R. Clark, *131*

Introduction

MY DAD ALWAYS TEASINGLY called it "poultry." That's kind of the attitude I had toward it when I was a kid, too. Poetry didn't seem to be much good for anything. But as I grew up and in deeper love with words, things shifted.

I don't remember the first time it happen, but I always know now when it does. It's what I call that poetry magic thing. The poem touches something inside your head or your heart, sends a shiver to your liver, and makes you say "Whoa" out loud in a soft spoken-to-yourself whisper.

Ever have one of those moments? That's what poetry is all about. Poems are condensed and distilled chunks of reality, boiled down to their most intense essence.

When you pour yourself into a poem, it's like when you pour water on one of those dried sponge toys – the little blue blob suddenly expands into a giant dinosaur or whatever. A good poem does that sort of thing in your head, expanding your insight and broadening your emotional sensitivities.

A way long time ago, my interest in poetry was first piqued by the likes of Rod McKuen and Kahlil Gibran. That interest was augmented by the music of Simon and Garfunkel, the Doors, Tim Hardin, Leonard Cohen, and others.

Fortunately, I had an English teacher in high school who nudged me toward more serious material. I started digging into e. e. cummings (not just the cute stuff), Robert Frost, John Leax, Carl Sandburg, Emily Dickinson, T. S. Eliot, Dylan Thomas, and others. Later in college, another teacher of English immersed me in Milton, Donne, and the other great older English poets.

My favorite poet is James Dickey. He died a few years ago. He was the author of *Deliverance* and even had a role in the movie that was based on his novel. I always experience that poetry magic thing when I read his poems, especially "Fence Wire." It pulls you in and you see and feel everything as if you are in the poem.

Another poet that I really like and just recently discovered is Stephen Dunn, a Pulitzer winner

All that's just to let you know that, while my poetry may not be as good as that of a Dickey or Dunn or whomever, I do know what good poetry is about.

When I write a poem, I try to write it well. Sometimes I succeed and sometimes flop miserably. You can read and decide for yourself which I've done with each of the poems in *The Godtouch*. My hope is that you'll find at least one that does that poetry magic thing to you.

Stephen R. Clark

The Godtouch was first published in 1985. All of the original 55 poems from 1985 edition of *The Godtouch* can be read online at: TheGodtouch.com.

Some of these poems have appeared previously in these magazines: alive now!, Bible Studies Magazine, Blue Unicorn, CAM, Christian Bookseller, Christian Herald, Christianity & Literature, College Poetry Review, The Disciple, Encore, Epiphany, Eternity, face-to-face, Freeway, HIS, The New York Poetry Forum, Pentecostal Evangel, Poetry Today, Wellspring, and Youth Alive!

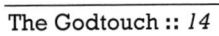

First Words
Original Foreword

THE POEMS in *The Godtouch* will provide a delightful experience for the connoisseur of good religious poetry. The reality and feeling that are so much a part of true religious experience are at the heart of each poem, but the vehicle of expression is contemporary and bold rather than sentimental and trite.

Stephen Clark is a young man of marked sensitivity in a variety of areas. His poetry is a copious response to his physical, emotional, and spiritual experiences. Occasionally traditional, but more frequently innovative, Mr. Clark expresses with strong feelings his moods of anger, nostalgia, faith, praise, and hope. The tone is tough or gentle, depending on the thought or feeling he is sharing.

Roots firmly planted in an evangelical Protestant tradition assure a solid familiarity with theological concepts and Biblical story. For readers acquainted with the historical tradition of religious poetry, the style of the poems in *The Godtouch* is reminiscent at times of the metaphysical style of some of the outstanding seventeenth century English religious poets. But the feel throughout is very contemporary. I highly commend Mr. Clark for his fine volume of poetry.

Dr. Zenas J. Bicket
Academic Dean, Evangel College
Springfield, Missouri, 1985

Part One

The Godtouch
The Forgetting Season

The Forgetting Season

THE summer mind greens thick
with the foliage of words and visions,
only to loose them
in the cool casual season
of a second's turning,
undiscerning
of their flashing beauty. . .

The bright thoughts
fall from the mind,
colorful invisibilities,
and in random heaps,
die.

The best thoughts, unwritten
always are forgotten.

Love & Wind & Innocence

It was the day of the big wind and you,
Lithe and supple, bending to the wind
In childish dance, eyes big and
Believing, dark-haired wonder, each strand
Alive to the will of the wind, swaying you in your
Big hat, twirling you in the grass, an
Imagined ballerina, not tiptoed but just
As graceful, lulling me to you, teasing
Me away, dancing with your shadow,
Making me jealous of it, wanting to be
Your only shadow, your only accompaniment,
Following you without running, inhibited
By my seriousness, playing the unplayful
Man, seeing you as a woman, on the day
Of the big wind and you, lithe and supple,
Bending to the wind, and to me.

Thumbs & Pulses

Two thumbs, then three, then four
Confused and lost from the proper
Hands, but oblivious to their
                displacement.
Two pulses, first separate and alone,
Emerge to merge. In counterpoint, investigate
New rhythms, realizing the other,
Then soloing, listening to the
Single beat of each.

                Love flows
Through those cadent veins ending in
Gentle percussion in the thumbs,
Touching. And two loves couple,
Become one, separate for a time to
Realize themselves, only to return
To each other, dependent and addicted
To the new eurhythmic communion.

Withstanding the Storm

WIND, like a crazed spirit,
Grapples through the trees
Stirring the leaves in a frenzied
Swirling madness and trailing them
In its endless wake.

We heard it coming,
From the other side of the small woods,
Where it crashed into the trees
After its long uncluttered run
Over the open fields beyond.

In the woods, it went crazy.
Its purposeful blowing
Diverted into a legion of twisting
Separate fierce gusts,
Entwining the branches invisibly,
Hissing like lunatic snakes.

We heard it coming
And knew the consequence
Of staying out in the open too long
In spite of the welcome coolness
Preceding its veiled velocity.

Besides the twigs and leaves
And dust that it threw up.
There was the skyfire behind it.
The clouds,
Black bellied and belching,
Boiling and churning insanely,
Turned the bright spaces
Between the clacking trees
Incredible dark, eclipsing day.

Inside the house, inside ourselves,
Our hearts beat fast
As the house groaned and wracked
Against the howling
And we waited,
To see if we would survive again,
Or this time, become ourselves, wind.

Last Days

BEYOND burning
the wet leaves steam
in the autumn rain rotting.

Rounds

The sun fails suddenly
Beyond the standard horizon
Springing dark upon us
Like a trap.
The moon comes out
And pokes around among the stars,
Glowering and full,
As haggard streaks of clouds race
Insanely across the foreboding apparition.
Quietly, we put on the masks,
Bringing our fears to the surface
In these horrific plastic expressions.
Bravely we clench our paper bags
And go out into this crazy
Halloween night.
Miniature spirits, imps, wildlings
Of questionable nature.
Friend or foe? Fearsome or funny?
Solemnly we collect
our various booty with some risk,
Making the rounds of the neighborhood,
And tracing our small anger on the windows
Dark and empty against us
With crayons of pure soap.
Then race home through the whirling leaves
Scared silly and laughing, anxious to
Eat the treats and tell the tales
of our treacherous tricks
And the stalking goblins
Sifting through the shadows, at our heels.

Tangled in Time

AGING:
        a memory larger
        than the mind

A boy in the skin of man.

Not yet feeling the sum total,
but still sensing
        those days:

Summer vacations & odd jobs
        & doing the circuit downtown
& girls
  with no strings

        But no

        no

Now
Older now
& older yet beyond . . .
     & strings . . .

Strings are webs infinitely spun.

& I am stuck
     with myself
     & aging

Romans 6 / for David Ralph Dodge
The Prankster: A Memorandum

DEATH
comes in the night
    as a thief,
   while you are up late,
    alone,
   writing poems about death.
and he unplugs your coffeepot
and tangles the typewriter ribbon,
   to remind you
   that he means business,
and is not joking
      as you are.

Afternoon, Fading

S̲HADOWS
sift into the room
and lie on everything like dust.

Fear & Loafing

I fear to write,
To poorly pen the words
That come too slow
Or not at all.
And so to calm the fears
That steel this foolish mind,
I loaf with pen in hand
And head declined.

Shut the Door Behind You

the season changes
with dramatic weather

a wet dark bleakness
shrouds the cooling days

the sunshine is going
out of our yellowed lives

and we move inside
awaiting the silent white

Part Two

The Godtouch
The Christmas Poems

1 John 3:18

Love Poem

Love
arrows
  through
by act and deed
    deep
      to the heart
        and the mind
   where words
   only
     touch
barely.

Philippians 2:15

The Star

Into cold space and endless emptiness,
    far within a deep indelible dark
where there was nothing but vacuum,
        the dump of despair and death,
  a small point of planted light grew.
    and came shining slowly
        with supreme and certain brilliance,
infusing a deep day and wide warmth,
    overcoming with simple sustaining surety
  the dark despondent depth . . .
            then
out of this nether of nothingness
    more stars appeared
        shining somewhat dimly,
  but shining steadily and growing.

burning within and reflecting the original star,
    these stars are one with the first
        and contain its fire within
           and reflect its presence without.

they
are son-stars, children of the original light.
and burning brilliantly,
            breaking from the dark depth,
    they spread into the indefinite infinity
          giving meaning and definition and form
                    to the limitless line of time
as universes
              galaxies
                    and constellations.
     they have moved into communities of light
          cohering and commingling
                    in cogent cooperation,
bringing white-hot truth and order and beauty
          into the midst of this rank darkness,
                    seeking intently to change it
     into one shining sheet
                    of pure eternal light.

The Shepherds

The night began as any other
night begins with darkness,
starred sky, and imploding
silence.
But the slow rising moon
was followed by a brighter star
that settled strangely low
over the glowing town beyond the rise.
This bright beaming newcomer
became the topic
of their quiet evening murmuring
as they sat glowing
around the warming fire.

Then the night dissolved in sudden terror
as the star seemed to fall
right on them, flashing huge
and hovering over their frightened
bowed and befuddled forms.
As they cowered, awestruck
and trembling against the frosted ground,
they heard voices.
Above their disbelieving heads,
the star was talking to them,
      singing to them,
inviting them to look up to see faces,
briefly, angels with a message.
Then nothing but silence blowing
over the low Christmas christened hills.

They rose, still trembling, stunned, awed,
and curious. They made their way,
wondering, sensing hope,
toward the soft glow of Bethlehem,
just below the beckoning star.

The Angels

The presses of heaven
were stopped.
The rumored event had happened,
and cherubim had the scoop.
It was Christmas for the first time.
And as if they couldn't wait
for the morning's first edition,
the angels burst brilliantly
over the front page of the sky
with a joyous banner headline
and a miraculous news story.
And the shepherds, like excited paperboys,
delivered the heralded word
from street corner to stable
as they made their way
to the scene of this sensational event.
And as they gazed at the child,
they kept one ear tuned toward the sky
just in case
late breaking additional information
was to come over the wire
from the choiring heavenly press room.

The Nativity

As helpless as he was,
he deserved more privacy.
Yet they gathered and stared,
not completely understanding what they saw,
just that they had to see ...

Mary was tired and sore and a little sick.
But she had heard the heralding angels
and knew they would come, that they had to come.
To see this new small life
that had been holy conceived inside her.
She did what she could to tidy the dusty stall,
putting fresh hay in the manger
and carefully wrapping the child
in her only spare clean skirt. There was no more,
for the time, to be done. She smiled bravely, trying
to look her best, trying to collect her thoughts
and slow her racing heart ...

Joseph stood by,
beside his beloved young wife,
uncertain how to act, how to stand.
He was a father, yet not a father.
He was proud of his brave Mary, and awed
by this birth. Just moments before
she had been wracked by the shrieking pains of labor.
And above her screams and sobs, he could have sworn he
heard singing. Voices, sweet like only voices
of angels could be. Then
the child's first gasping cries
crashing against the impinging darkness.
He wasn't sure he would ever understand
what was taking place, and not sure he wanted to.
Shifting his weight, he stood silent,

his brow creased in thought, watching
the gathering people ...

The shepherds, gesturing from stall to sky,
began talking in quick, excited words
about what they had seen and heard in the hills.
How night turned to noon,
and of angel choirs singing tidings of joy
and birth, and the child, found just as was promised,
small, red, and wrinkled, sleeping next
to cattle and chickens ...

It was all too amazing. Yet,
he lay quietly dozing, having just been fed,
not totally unaware of the world,
but not more so than any other newborn.
He deserved more privacy.
Yet they would never leave him alone.
But always come to him, time after time,
to adore and obey, or to mock and kill,
as the paradox of Christmas
began burning in their hearts.

The Wisemen

Miniature magi march majestically
down the middle aisle of the church
mistakenly placed in the annual
Christmas pageant.
They really came two years later
to give their gifts and long considered
adoration to the patient child.
But in our modern reenactment
of this eternal event,
the kings come to the stable
along with the sheep and the shepherds.
God doesn't mind
this once-every-year-error,
because the message is still clear.
Magic is vanquished by the intense reality
of this fragile fatal incarnation
worshipped in remembrance
at every church that is our Bethlehem.
Bathrobe wrapped wisemen
bearing gifts of gold painted cardboard
and mom's empty perfume bottles
make up an inexact scene.
But draw us just as strongly just the same,
to that holy point beneath the star
that burns His perfection into our hearts,
daily becoming His wisemen.

The Fool

SATAN sank deeper into
his insidious insane stupor.
Ravaging monstrous rage ripped
at the dead flesh of his senseless heart.
He summoned all his forces
to the small congested town.
With each turning away
and shut inn door,
he frothed in wicked glee.
But he forgot the stables
and the empty stalls.

      The couple bedded down
and the pains came closer and sharper.
In distant fields beyond the city's glow
angelic hosts were singing praises.
The child was born. Shepherds
and magi were on the way.
And Satan screamed unholy terror
storming shrieking through his
dismal madhouse kingdom,
knowing, but refusing like a fool
to admit that all was more lost
than ever before.

Prayer at Midwinter

GOD
* * * * *

infinitely starred
General
    of my
        celestially aimed
            soul
Please
i pray You, Sir

Command one
sergeant angel
      with white flaming wings
     to come
and touch our humble house
       with warmth,
and
unfreeze
       our useless, insubordinate
          water pipes.

Amen.

Watching Snow

      WHITE fat frozen flakes fly flailing,
evading, dodging each other in the air,
                              trying to find
                              just
                              their
                              spot.
A frenzied dance of pure white madness,
      each flake careens insanely, feverishly
                            to the ground
          and explodes into the rest.
In the mind
          there is a constant *plssh!*
    plssh!
          plssh! while watching this
                wild ballet.

But outside the skull is only silence,
      (like cotton stuffed in the ears)
                              and white*
            And white*
                      And white*

                      *
                          *
                  *

Winter, Snow & Cold

WRAITHS of vagrant steam
grey into the air
	from gutter drains
and mouths.

	Sounds haunt the blowing silence.
Words hang in the cold
and end.
	Snow sucks all noise down.

When you break the frozen crust
	with a step, it's all released
like the sigh of ghosts.

	Your feet become numb
	as the wetness melts in
	bringing the cold home.

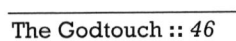

Part Three

The Godtouch

Seasonal Hell

Seasonal Hell

BURN this night
      awake and tossing
     holding the fierceness
       of the sun
in the sizzling of your skin

You are wrapped in the heat of your folly
     and glow softly red in your bed
       trying to escape the pain
     by sinking into the dream
of thinking and believing

"Next week, I *will* be cool again,
and won't peel, but be tan!"

Greeting & Confirmation

ON mornings when wakened by only the sun
And the soft sounds of early morning;

> *My own metric breathing in whispers,*
> *The singing of the water pipes,*
> *A bird in debate with itself.*

My mind fills slowly with gentle clarity
As the presence of the Lord is known
By His voice which moves on my being;

> *No explosive manifestations,*
> *No banging cymbals or flashing lights,*
> *Just His still small voice of love;*

"Good morning, my child, my son."

Remodeling

    i was
    an empty house

my plumbing was out of order;
        my wiring
  had short-circuited;
     & my foundations were crumbling;
& the yard
     was overgrown
     with weeds & weeds & weeds;
yet
& Yet He bought this
    wasting piece
    of junk real estate
    as is
    & moved in right away (!)

then
& Then
O Yes! & THEN . . .

. . . brand new bright brilliant wallpaper & paint
     on all the old grey insides;
& all new modern top-quality permanent siding
     all around the outside;
& new pipes & new wiring & a solid foundation . . .

   . . . everything & everything is new!

           is reclaimed!
                    is fixed!
&, (i've been told),
       as long as He stays

      i
      with HIM
      am priceless
           (!)

Backyards: Summer: Night

At night
    when all is medium cool
        in summer
            lights fly
and sentence out the air
        with Morse.
  And voices drift
        like Frisbees of sound
between the yards
    between the murmurs of air conditioning fans,
coming from the golden glowing porches
      where life exists in the dark,
  in the yellow shimmerings
        of concrete slab oases,
where messages of intent are passed
    in the supple movements
        of the sun struck golden bodies
    in the haltered swaying
        of liberated breasts
      and in the ice rattling gestures
of liberal minded men
    circumscribing their fragile realities.
From yard to yard
    the only life making sense
        are the small dark voices
           playing and pretending
    chasing flying lights
        and each other
      at night
    when all is medium cool
        in summer.

Night Sketch: Heat & Rain

1.

The sounds of thunder and rain moving away
Confuse with the sound of the fan
Rumbling uselessly in the window.

The light of my lamp mingles
With the fading lightning emphasizing
In needless punctuation,
The embracing heat.

Shadows curl around the room
And lie in the corners
Like sleepy, sulking cats.

2.
This summer night clings viciously
To its day collected heat,
Eluding the cooling of the evening rain.

Instead of relief, there is only steam,
Stretching lazily along the gleaming streets
Where constellations of streetlights
Are captured in puddles on black pavement:

A cheap imitation of the infinite night
Hidden behind the black and grey
Bellowing bellies of emptied clouds.

Night as Child

HEAR into the quiet here,
Knowing it's not really,
But only an illusion of quiet,
With noise pushed off into the distance,
But not over the edge
Of far enough,
And muffled by the silken moonlight.
                              Nightness
Settles into you with the rhythmic
Unresounding pounding factory,
And the hushless rush of distant traffic,
Mixed into the crickets' ceaseless chirping,
And the foggy breathing
Of the forest's sleeping monsters
Menacing softly
In your favorite fearful dreams.

Matthew 18:1-6 / for Mom, Dad, and Sis
The Fear of God

THE night is hushed.
And I feel small and alone
under the covers in my roomworld.
Outside across the steaming street
the insects sing click-silver songs
below the glass-skinned sky.
My gnomish heart tocks tombishly
as shadowed shapes stalk
in the darkness at the edge of the bed
playing with the dustballs underneath.
Slowly the eyeball moon moves over
and shines dimly around the rolling room
waking the ghosts in the cross-backed chairs.

It is Sunday night.
And my heathen head is unhinged
heaving with "Holy! Holy! Holy!" armed angels chanting.
And the preacher's images of hell and demons
and Armageddon's rancid red rivers.
I lay remembering the tripping little lies,
the wicked thoughts,
and the mean things spoken and done,
and become frightened.
If my lamplighting Christ came now
with silver trumpet bursting sound,
would I be stranded on my island bed
in the drifting darkness?

The night's silence accuses sharply.
Full of damning desperation and darts of doubts,
I fear that at the other end of the long-halled home
my parents are not there. Taken. Changed. Twinkling.
And HE has returned, leaving me, lackluster, tarnished,
in this deafening, frenzied hush.
Nearly too scared, yet pricked by need,
seeking certainty in the face of fallen fear,
I touchdown on the floor. Reassured, finding only carpet
and cold wood, I creep down the hallowing hall
cursing childishly every creak, fearing finding nothing,
or being found out.

At their door, always open, I wait,
listening for breathing or snoring, then look,
and they are there! Love lumps on the moonlit bed!
I still have a changeling's chance
to make things right again,
and stop by the bathroom, relieved to be relieved.
Then bumble back to bed
with only fears of dark and night things going bump,
and a prayer of repentance in my whistling heart,
not often enough again fearing
in quite the same intense way
the chastening chance of being missed and left alone,
in the chilling stillness, lost,
like a child in the dangling dark.

Lord, have mercy.

Advertising

lots of people
puttin' Jesus on their
jeans
instead of in their
hearts
they don't love him
they just wear him

Part Four

The Godtouch
Easter Poems

The Runner

RUNNING,
Moving smoothly along an empty beach
Early in the morning misty thick
With spring warmth, a pre-dawn dewy haze,
You can hear his breathing
In timed panting with his feet's
Sandy slapping, leaving wet impressions
Trailing him
Running,
Moving his legs in ecstatic delight,
Enjoying the feel of his muscles,
Taut and working,
Moving him, pushing him,
Through the glowing dawn, the salt air.
Above him
Gulls in white swirls
Cry out his presence to the day,
To the sleeping sea.
Running,
Arms taut and solid by his sides,
Moving in balanced rhythm,
His head up, smiling open and large,
Intense in his celebration
And worship, he runs.
In solitude, Jesus runs.

Christ Came Down, Arising

I will cling to the old rugged cross,
Bloodstained timber, slowly rotting,
My hopes are pinned there, and
I cling and cannot let go.
My Savior bids me move away,
But I'm not sure. In the cross,
I have security. A sense of permanence.
Away from the cross are only His promises.
I can feel and see the precious cross.
It's more than a mere symbol.
This image of tortured death is my only reality.
Its shadow covers me, and I've grown used
To the pain of the splinters,
And its oppressive weight.
It is my only comfort, even though
My Lord says He will carry it for me.
And others pass me by,
Whispering what good kindling it would make.
Their voices are demons hissing.
I shake the darkening doubts they stir up,
And cling ever tighter to my old rugged cross,
Watching the Lord walk away, beyond the rise.

The Betrayal

Kissed, he gave himself gently
Into the hands of those who came for him.
Armed and shielded, they looked and felt foolish,
Capturing this man, standing unflinching
In front of them.
    His followers fled, fearful,
And he blessed them, understanding,
Knowing in time they would return to him,
Better men, broken by this one moment
Of reasonable disgrace.
    He stood silent and stared.
A piercing peaceful gaze
That none could endure or resist.
    It made them nervous,
And fanned the small embers
Of restless anger inside them.
    They scurried around him,
Trying to create an illusion of capture.
They were unsure of why they were taking him.
But they needed no reason. The night
Was tempered with irrational tension.
    Cowering in the shadows behind the others,
Judas followed, whimpering, wiping
Frantically at his lips, burning,
As if he'd tasted acid. And all around him
In the maddened darkness, he heard the
Heckling shrill laughter of delighted demons,
And the rattling of silver coins.

The Shining

THREE of them,
Profiled against the bruised sky.
Deformed, misused trees
Burdened with a trilogy of lives
Hanging like broken, discarded dolls.
And the load was lightening
Moment by moment.
    Soon there would be nothing left
But the blood stains,
The clinging central memories,
And the rough-hewn symbol
Of an empty cross.
    For three days despair dripped down
From the rain bleeding skies
And soaked into the perplexed hearts
Of eleven aching men and others.
    Then the Word shone brilliantly
Burning away the mists
As the warm reality of His promise
Began to soothe their troubled hearts.
    The tomb was empty.
Memories became again an encounter
With reality as He came among them.

    Three of them
On the road to Emmaus
Profiled against the diminishing horizon.
Two with hearts aflame in anticipation,
And One, resurrected, that caused these
Blind to surely see, and the eleven
To multiply the truth
Of Christ in us,
Alive!

The Taking

UNTOMBED Lord,
He descended deliberately
Hade's corkscrew steps
Into the mortified midst
Of startled flinching demons screaming,
Scurrying blindly,
Cowering in anguish
Behind their now coward master.
    Satan writhed nervously, hissing,
Growling and groveling, cornered,
As the true King appeared
In stinging silver brilliance
To take from Satan with simple strength
The keys to stenched death's domain.
    And then ascend
With grace and joy and song,
Shaking the earth aware,
To appear again, shining,
To men, and claim their taunted souls
Anew with gentleness, power,
And love.

The Point

THE star shone streaming light,
        an upside-down point

  of exclamation,
           as God
           became
           incarnate,
to live a brief
world jolting paragraph
        as whole man
         among puzzled men,
         to hang suspended
like a broken off
sentence
as the elements around Him
provided a graphic
        punctuation of promise.
Then,
three days later,
a still stone now moved
(like my heart)
was the point
of His ascending exclamation
    and
      the period
      of absolute certainty
      for the fact of our
      imperfect unfinished
      faith, becoming ...

Wood to Flesh

Wood
to flesh
rough
& splinters
breaking
skin to blood
staining
wood
with life
for our
life to be
more than
a log
in the eye
& a thorn
in the
flesh

First Easter Morning

first Easter morning/
    the cock
    crows.

& Death's
    denied.

Luke 19:45-47a; 1 Corinthians 3:16,17

Cleansing of the Temple

My soul was merchandise
        ripped in several pieces
  and sold to anyone
      who would pay.
My fragmented life was passed
   from buyer to buyer
      to be used at their will
    and discarded
        by resale.
I could never be my own owner.
Then
    Jesus, at my asking,
stormed into my life and heart
    and scourged the evil there
    and threw out those wicked powers
       who bartered for my soul
and sought to sell me
       into eternal miserable bondage.
He cleansed this fleshly temple
    and bought all the pieces of my life
  with His
      and made me whole
one with Him
       and set His Holy Spirit in me
  daily teaching me
  how to be His holy temple.

Part Five

The Godtouch
The Hunt

The Hunt

L‍ord
our lives have
come in line
like the hinter's
eye through
the scope
marking the point
of death on a
wild life

God Even Gideon

G<small>OD</small>
even gideon
had doubts
and sought certain certainty
fleecy white sureness
even this
holy hero of the motel
chains
wanted to be sure
you were really on
his side
and behind him
1,000%

so it is so
bad for me
if i ask you
for something
more concrete
more solid
more graspable
than wonder
and second-
hand faith?

Matthew 8:28-34; Mark 5

Relocation

"A change of address
              now is in effect."
The demons stare
into the vacant red
            valentine-shaped soul
in disbelief
      and laugh, reading the blood-penned
          notice;
"Former occupants will now reside
            in the local swine,
         somewhere soon,
     underwater . . ."
Then suddenly scream in furious maniac rage
          as a formless frenzy
              takes them.
Other-willed, they are moved, repelled,
        maddened and squealing,
swallowing warm lake water,
            choke and sink,
the note ending, "The King, now residing."

Dry Tinder Quenched

fire
is not
image enough
to equal
that burning
of His
tinder love
in the kindling
heart
of the newborn
soul

Laughing Savior

Christ came juggling
    into my life
      took my doubts
  my fears and failures
     took all my sins
and tossed them
        round and round
    casually in the air
  and with the touch
        from his nimble fingers
turned each one into something shining
         glowing
           silver
    and gave these feelings back
     as peace
       joy
     love and hope
and with a laugh
      breathed upon me
  and sent the Spirit to me
  filling me with smiles
      and praise

The Incoming

EMPTINESS
echoes
with hollow
depth.

& need of filling
is seed of desire for it.

The Spirit echoes not,
But resounds within.
Filling unlike in pouring
    from the bottom up
But as vacuum overcome
& instantly negated

      with an incredible affirmation
      of wholeness, acceptance & love.

Romans 8:26
Maintenance

Internal pain
& confusion
a combustible unstable
mixture
igniting improperly
with anger & frustrations
misfiring
& stalling
the processes
of living/being
the spirit sputtering
to God
for new fuel
& fresh oil
to keep the heart
burning
the gears turning
but words
evade the prayer
& problems choke
the voice
until the Spirit
speaks for you
tripping the foreign
words from your lips
as smoothly
as the purring
of a rotary engine

exclaiming precisely
your need of a tune-up
to God
as the brakes
are unclenched
& the hands raise
in praise
& the gears shift
into place
as you wheel
into the Kingdom's garage
before the Master Mechanic

for Harrie Maat
Hymn

i would sing
of darkness
come out of . . .
& sorrow
that pierced
to the heart's
secret center
turned to
inexplicable joy . . .
& pain
sharp & critical
raging in a wracked
body burning
to understand why
answered with the
greater mystery
of the soul's
deep healing &
the mind's restoration
to peace . . .
& i would sing
of HIM

Praise

O INFINITESIMAL God
      great and wondrous God
    Thou art in the majestic smallness
      of the minute molecule
& the exquisite simplicity
      of the squiggly amoeba
        & the perfect precision
   of the porcupine's prickly points
& the Source of the force
        that drives the small
    wild creatures
      of the forest
    to have being

and we
are more valuable
      than many sparrows
   in Your eyes
O most infinite Father
     Our Father

for Rev. Paul Davidson
Masonry

laying
block upon
tenuous
    block
we pray
for strength to hold true
until the mortar
of faith
    becomes firm
and solid
as we are made daily
into
the Holy Temples
    of our Lord

Part Six

The Godtouch
Leavings

"Departure rehearses death." John Updike

Leavings

I.

GOMER left Hosea
Panting after adulterous lovers.
The prodigal left home
Tramping after cheap thrills.
And I walked away from You
Into adulterous and apostate imaginations.
Lives like table scraps,
Leavings to be disposed of,
To rot, to decay,
These departures led into dying.
The death of dreams and hope,
And self.

II.
Like Gomer on the block
Shackled by her own disillusionment;
Like the prodigal among swine
Groveling in senseless despair
After feeding his soul on garbage;
I came seeking undeserved mercy,
Knowing in some deep memory
That You would still be there
To buy me back from my demon master.
Not with silver and barley, but blood,
And heal my fragmented being,
Clothing me in the many colors or Your love.

Recovery

R‍ENDERED helpless
again
& barely hoping on
      faded faith
Feeling left
        dangling
        in mid-life
        to slowly
   twist
 in bitter winds
   of
discontent & dissolution
    when
 His voice moves out
  into the center
    of this
 tempering tempest
touching the turmoil
into stillness by loving
    degrees
    until
    it is
    peace
    again

in the mind & heart
relief & sobbing joy
    lifts
  He   this
as   dangling
                  battered
                      man
to a solid standing
healing fevered faith
& broken spirit into
rejoicing whole hope
again & again . . . . .

Hallelujah!
        Amen.

Moment of Always Meeting

IN silence. In between the whispers
Of indistinct night sounds.
When the world nearest me is quiet,
                    is dark.
And I sit in the midst of this near,
Encircling stillness,
                it is here,
In this moment,
As I read & pray & am still,
That I find you waiting for me.
To just sit with me & be with me awhile.
We sit, just loving each other.
And we talk, softly. Gesture. Share. Laugh.
        And you touch me sometimes,
Leaning toward me, knowing me.
The good, the bad, the obscure & the hurt.
You know as no one can know
And you accept as no one can accept.
        You speak
And your voice is the silence
Distilled from the passing thunder.
Intense absolute gentle quietness.

      You forgive the wrongs.
The stumblings.
You correct & firmly scold,
With tears.
And I, with tears, am sorry.
You touch away the pain & calm the hectic heart.
And we rejoice inside this sleeping home.
      In foreign whispers, praise.
Then you rise, place your hand on my shoulder.
You pray for me. Pull me up & hug me
As a friend met after years away.
(And it's always like this.)
You bid farewell and leave
Without leaving . . .

. . .The night is still night
   And still quiet. And this moment
   Just as all moments,
   Is not empty.

for Zenas J. Bicket
In Silence Singing

In the silence
of a world
gone deaf and dumb
stupid & blind
the best minds stumbling
on half-truths
& whole lies
having negated God neatly
by dialogue & debate
believing in nothing

& so doing everything mindlessly

mindless of the light
& sound of truth
singing & shining
from the pages of the prophets & poets
whose pens are powered by the God who is

the pens that pour out
page after page
of truth
in images
of hope
of whole minds
healed of love
in the face
of nothing
but despair

we are
    in the silence singing   Jesus cares &
                                      we care!
                into a world
                        gone deaf & dumb
              stupid & senseless
                          we sing our words
His Word
      onto the pages knowing & believing
in the simple sometimes of miracles
                  of hearing & seeing

for Laurel and the "old gang"

A Step is not a Leap

Everything is out of focus
Looking through screen doors.
You struggle to control and
Reconcile the images beyond.
But you can't.
Everything is rough-edged,
Blurred.
Reality seems out of focus.
You get the feeling that to step
Out past the screen door
Would be to enter
A sort of twilight zone.
Stepping into . . . what?
Maybe more of a leap
Across an imagined chasm of fear
Into the seeming unknown of life?
A parallel here
Between thought and vision.
What you see is out of focus.
What you know seems uncertain, not easily
Verified. And until the screen door
Is opened, the blur of uncertainty
Will persist.
But yet, while the vision is not
Perfect, you still see
And you know what the images represent.
The leap is not blind.
Just impaired. And leaping into
Faith, as opening a screen door,
Is stepping into joyful clarity.

You knew it all along.

for Robert Stephen Dicken
The Sickness

A TUMOR of hope grows
terminally
in the depths of my being.
And in my despair, it burns.
I hope, I aspire.
Morbid prognoses denied,
visions persist to plague
my merciless memory.
Torn and bleeding, I rise,
take up my bed,
go on, incurable.

for Francis A. Schaeffer
The Godtouch

                he suffers
tied to infinity
                with the voice of God instilled
deep in his singing brain
                sounding to the heart
burning and enlarging
                with the Godtouch

time and space flow through him
                threading him thoroughly
onto the web and weave
                of incarnate history

cross-eyed vision
                tongue-tied in the Spirit
he's an unstilled laborer
                tilling the weed-wracked fields
of a fruitless justice
                with hands calloused yet gentle
and a voice that cracks
                the deepest night
he speaks and infinity echoes
                around him
confirming his ever-widening reality

cursed with a blessing of too accurate vision
words draw him closer
      to his final apocalypse
as eternity awaits
   at the end of the ever firm arm
     to pull him to the bosom
       the Source
    &
    final comfort

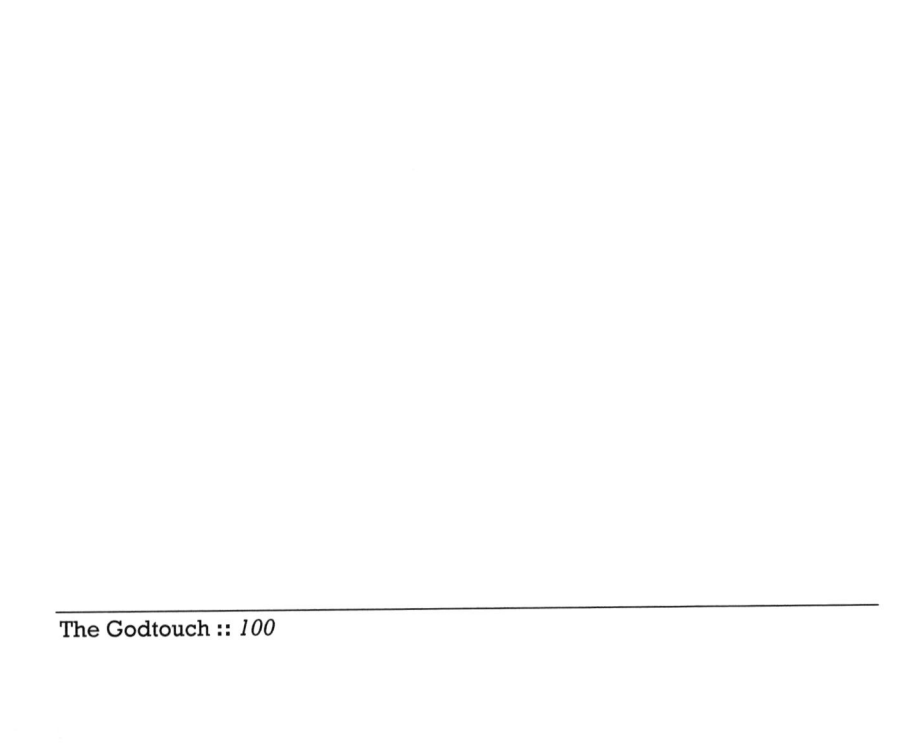

Part Seven

The Godtouch

More

Wound

to write
too deep
is to wound
the soul
with a wound
that will not heal
but
only grow...

Bad Ending

TWILIGHT ensconces the remnants
   of scattered pieces of clouds
      floating on the oil skinned sky
         flame bright streaks
           burning the day down to a nub
      final sparks ember on the horizon
   turning on or into stars flying up
hot white spots on black canvas
   the moon becomes bigger
      grinning shadows onto the earth
   trees angle limbs like flailing arms
gray old men standing lost in yards
   joints clacking and complaining against the wind
cold dandruff falls scattering across the grass
   dark greenless carpeting under snow
        in a window a lamp lights a sunrise of
     flame
     glowing into an empty room
     where no one waits
   for the return.
The world is lost.
The fire is burning.
Ashes.
Ashes.
All fall down.

Dreamsong / Nightsong

CRISP moonlight
chromes the cool air

smoke sifts up like
silt from burning leaves

lamp lit shadows gouge
gaping slots in the moon hazed night

(black holes in sleep
to slip through into unreality)

becoming a vagabond
in your own dream

you tramp the night
to its too soon waking

unresolved
                and aching...

When Night Falls

If the day falls to night, will it hurt me?

If it falls, will it fall like snow
and melt from the heat of my touch?

If it falls, will it fall like rain,
and gently caress my face as it leaves
a sheen of cool moisture?

If it falls, will it fall like tears,
warm and salty on my trembling lips?

If it falls, will it fall like hail,
and sting sharply before bouncing
away, hard and harsh?

If it falls, will it fall like autumn leaves,
colorful and rustling beneath my feet?

If the day falls to night, will it hurt me?

Or will it close quietly around me
like a warm comforter on a cold day?

Or will it just mean that the sun is gone
and the night has come?

Dark. Will it hurt me?

Some

The light fades.
The air cools.
Most go in
To the arms of another.

Some just go in.
Some just go.

Christmas Trinity

CHRISTMAS comes each year
birthing Christ anew in our hearts,
exploding hope in joyous caroling
echoing down snow paved streets.

We greet each other with gifts of smiles
made of unwrapped teeth and
seasoned words of cheered blessing.

Children guessing at secrets
held captive in red wrapped presents,
giggle and muffle squealing anticipation
while looking skyward for angels,
wondering about Santa's reality.

Congeniality and peace bookend
the world as the specter of Christ's
birth hovers behind our festive facade.

God seeks faithful hearts aflame with truth,
seasoned saints seeking Him and serving
each other in love and devotion, honoring
the Spirit, the Giver, and the Given of Christmas.

Nice Ice

LIGHT
    flying
        bright
            brilliant
                dazzled
            day
        down
shattering
        shimmering
                on snow
            and ice
        froze your face
        glowing
like an open empty
refrigerator.

I know
because you gave me an ice cube
                for a kiss.

Epiphany Eidolic

ACROSS, beyond the haze of glass
A swollen dot of moon erupts,
And skates above the snowy sea
Of earth in winter slumbering.

I lie in bed and watch the night
Come through my window, burning bright.
This vision bursts into the air
And falls like dust motes everywhere.

I rise to touch the fallen dust
And know the knowing that I must,
Yet nothing meets my reaching hand,
But puddled moonlight on the stand.

I smile at my inventive mind,
And go to sleep, behind the blind.

Affirmations Against Aloneness

Yes,
The wind,
It rages
Against the warmth
And
Foretells
The coming
Of freezing storm.

Yes,
My cat,
She lies here
Wrapped in purring,
Close
Beside
My feet, full
Of dreams, stirring.

Yes,
Candles
Are burning
Against the dark
And
Alone
Coldness of
Being apart.

Clue

SOMEWHERE
There are two people

Facing each other in a café
At this very moment

They are drinking dark coffee
And they are saying nothing

And they have been saying nothing
For so long

They have forgotten why
They are together in the café

And they are waiting
For a clue.

Misfit

WHY do you believe that this is the truth?
Because I must. It is.
Why? How do you know?
It's there. Right there. Out in the open.
So?
Can you deny it? Do you deny it?
Yes. It is what you make of it. And I make of it nothing.
That's absurd! It is what it is!
Not so. I think it's all rather silly.
You would. That lets you off the hook.
Why would I want to be on it?
To be a real person. So that I could love you.
Love is a choice. Simply choose to do it with me.
I can't.
Why?
The truth?
Yes. Of course.
How would you know it if I told you?
Ah. I see. Then, goodbye.
Yes.

If, Then, Instead

if life was heaven on earth
if life was like a day at the beach
if life was like living on the leisure edge
if life was soft like butter
if life was sweetened cereal

instead of butter on toast burnt falling butter side down
instead of sand on the shore sore hot against bare soles
instead of edged like a razor shaving against skin's grain
        leaving us redfaced and raw
then
    it would be lived courageless
    unlearning
    stunted
for comfy cushioned existence
is not life
but a life sentence
    paroleless stupidity
    demeaning
    pointless
    hell
    ish

Tears of Fire

Hold life lightly
as if it could not even be touched
your fingers barely feeling
the warm vibration of it
as it moves through time
enveloping all in its path
crumbling creation to dust

Hold life lightly
let it touch you with no
more weight than a butterfly
or hummingbird
with wings flailing
ready to fly off at the slightest
jar

Hold life lightly
let it not hold you
or it will clasp you too tightly
so that you cannot breath
or see
or speak the truth

Hold lightly this life
and cling instead
to what comes after
for where your heart is
there is your treasure

You can spend it now
or possess it later

Hold life lightly now
or hold nothing
in death
but death
and tears of fire

The Secret of Being

She aches with his contagion.
He lives within his aging.
The moon becomes their falling
Spreading silver below her lying,
As though she were one being
Alive to him like no other.

She climbs the night exalted
Becoming the movement inside it.
The heat of her life is unwinding
Like flesh on a stick of pure burning.
And all that she does is for being,
On fire of green beginning.

Song is the outside of movement.
She sings in this dawning of time
As the moon burns silver to day.
The whispers of love fall below them
As though there were nothing to hear.
The secret of being is held
Alive to her like no other.

Roads

It's not sin if it's not wrong.
It's not wrong if it's not sin.

Right is righteousness lived out.
Wrong is righteousness ignored.

Christ is the way of righteousness.
Sin is the way of death.

All roads do not lead to the same end.
Absolutely.

Pied Piper

play me a wind song
between your lips
a whistle
blow me a sweet kiss
with a tune
musical love
hold my hand
in the dark
push my fears aside
with a movement of your mouth
keep me company
throw me your heart
with a breezy melody

play me a wind song
between your lips
a whistle

from a discussion of a short story, *A&P*, by John Updike

A Lecture on Advanced Writing Techniques

money sings after you've done it long enough
                    i couldn't help notice
the last complete paragraph on page 41
                    the herrings in a bag and twists its neck
sexual implications I'm sure
                    his facial look
sad sunday school superintendent stare
                    the handling of dialogue
he said she replied
                    ending up grabbing the thesaurus
almost goes further than is normally acceptable
                    expressed verbally
uh character sheets
                    assuming he had heard our lecture
none
                    they fulfill a similar function
an alternative to sammy
                    sammy feels the crowd
does he at the end
                    queenie
a terrific detail
                    he's at the next stall waiting on customers
stupid description

                lucinda
I don't know
                general america
you can say the same thing about any character
                may have just been one of those things that
came to his mind
I don't want to argue with you
                that's the academic policy
what others want is juvenile delinquency
                probably an example of my denseness

Together. Very.

Do you think?
Not really. Why should I?
Oh, I don't know. I just thought...
Did you? Or did I through you?
I'm not sure I get your meaning.
If there is any to get.
Stop. You're weirding me out.
I can't. I have to. It's my nature, you know.
I know. But I don't like it.
But I love you.
Hmmmm. Me too.
Love yourself? Or me?
Good question! Both I suppose.
You don't know?
I'm not sure what I know.
But do you think you know what you need to.
Yes. And I need you. Now.
I'm here.
Very.

With All My Strength

LISTEN to me breathe
as I lay still on my bed.
It is you that I'm breathing in
and not you that I am breathing out.
      Do you hear me?

Listen to me whisper
as I sit here quietly beside you.
These are my thoughts and desires of you
that I whisper into your ears.
      Are you listening?

Oh the intense sweetness of your presence
as you walk, sit, exist dearly near to me
talking and laughing and being.
      You are.

I listen to you and take your words in,
deeply.
      You fill my senses.
You fill my life.
You fill my heart with more
love than I can barely hold.
And I love to hold your love
      in my heart
   in my mind
in my whole being.
With all my strength.

It Rattles

It rattles.
The head, the heart,
the ground you stand on
falls away beneath your perception
as that which once held all things firm
crumbles into molecules of floating
doubts and fears and broken promises and
dreams fail to move you forward together,
now only one whole person leaving
behind you the scraps of failed hope
the puzzled pieces of an experiment
that did not pan out as so many
thought would happen,
the one that left alone in another's
life looking for what has been given up
and tossed aside becoming wasted
and rattled.

Jeremiah 4:3
Hearts of Steel

LIGHT flows around us and we are not enlightened.
Fire burns near us and we are not warmed.
Voices call to us and we are not hearing.
Wheels roll under us and we are not moved.
Visions pass over us and we are not seeing.
God walks besides us and we are not believing.

Girded with hearts of steel we live in our illusion
Of self-imposed importance. Gods for the Moment, we walk proudly into the doom of
An eternity unexpected and unprepared for.
Voices fill our ears with sweet lies and deceptions.
Light flows around us bathing us in darkness.

God walks away
and we don't care.

Haiku Ramblings

CICADA I
Sleeping underground
you sense the sleepy silence
of summer, then rise.

CICADA II
Your skin shed clings on
as you crawl higher or fly.
Stop. Coded buzzing.

CICADA III
Summer mercury,
blood red, filling the glass tube,
brings heat and your song.

CICADA IV
Aliens beneath
naked summer feet and sun
awake and conquer.

CICADA V
Strange skins cling on trees,
witness of resurrection
from years underground.

CICADA VI
Like us you live most
asleep in the darkened earth
awakening late.

DIVORCE I
You are wrong of course
to leave and then disappear
from even my dreams.

DIVORCE II
You banish yourself
from accountability
and my love. Goodbye.

DIVORCE III
You thought that he would
give you something more than what
I could give you. Well?

DIVORCE IV
You lied about what
we had and instead you ran
to what was not yours.

ARGUING
Words spill unceasing
and fall like frothing foam that
is flushed down the bowl.

FORSAKEN
Left to wilt, decay
is the hallmark of yielding
to your tender care.

CHANGE
Sometimes it happens
till it becomes who you are
but then means nothing.

SPAM
Unbidden it comes.
Penis will grow and riches
too. Only ten bucks.

SPRING TEASE
The sun breaks through clouds
that dissipate at their touch.
Warmth vamps green grass up.

RETICENCE
I am not seen here.
Invisible transparent
see-through soul awaits.

About the Author

Stephen R. Clark is a member of the Evangelical Press Association, the National Association of Evangelicals, and the principal of CleverSmith™ Writing (www.CleverSmith.com) in Oreland, Pennsylvania, as well as the writer of the award-winning blog, FaithBraised™ (www.FaithBraised.com). He has been writing for more than forty years.

He has authored short stories, poetry, online content, ad copy, scripts, speeches, direct mail, feature articles, and so much more. He has also ghostwritten several Christian books including *Preparing for Battle* by Mark Bubeck (Moody Press). He has contributed chapters to compilations, devotionals, and other books including the *NIV Men's Devotional Bible* (Zondervan) and *Inside Mysteries of the Bible* (Time & American Bible Society).

He released his first full-length novel, an award-winning thriller, *The Hungering Dark: Awakening* (WestBow Press) in the summer of 2016.

You can visit his personal web site at www.StephenRClark.com where you can learn more about him and his other books. He is joyfully married to BethAnn Clark, and they are members of Huntingdon Valley Presbyterian Church in Huntingdon Valley, Pennsylvania.

He also walked on fire. Once.

Follow Stephen online at these social media sites:

www.twitter.com/stephenrclark
www.facebook.com/StephenRClarkWriter
www.linkedin.com/in/stephenrclark

Also by Stephen R. Clark

From Epiphany Lane™ Press:

Home Noise: new poems

Christmas Believe: A Story of Joy & Wonder (A novella)

All Writing Is Not Equal: How To Write Anything Better

Pastor's Complete Model Letter Book

Words for Fall: Writings for the Season

Words for Winter: Writings for the Season

Words for Spring: Writings for the Season

Words for Summer: Writings for the Season

Words for All Seasons (combining all 4 of the above in one volume)

From other publishers:

A Cup of Comfort Devotional | Adams Media
(with Jim Bell)

Christian Miracles | Adams Media
(with Jim Bell)

Christian Family Guide to Surviving Divorce | Alpha
(with Pam Weintraub)

NIV Men's Devotional Bible | Zondervan
(Contributor)

Inside the Mysteries of the Bible | Time & American Bible Society
(Contributor)

Award-winning fiction:

The Hungering Dark: Awakening | WestBow Press
(a division of Zondervan & Thomas Nelson)

epiphany lane press

Made in the USA
Columbia, SC
20 December 2017